JIG FOR JOHN

Jon Jeffrey Grier

50410010

Jig for John
for Flute and Piano

Jon Jeffrey Grier

Flute

Flute

JIG FOR JOHN

Jon Jeffrey Grier

50410010

3
Flute

50410010

Selected Flute Publications

METHODS

BAKER, JULIUS
Cox, Alan

10300130 Daily Exercises for the Flute (Grade 4)

A terrific and valuable collection of exercises for advanced flutists, the studies in this book are intended to build a high degree of technical solidity by means of intensive work on scale, scale patterns, seventh-chord progressions, thirds, sixths, chromatic sequences, fast staccato, high tones, and various duet selections. By diligent and careful work on these daily exercises, students will build a flawless tehcnical foundation on the flute, and more advanced players will keep themselves in shape.

COLLECTIONS

BALENT, ANDREW

50341003 Classical Solos (Grade 2.5)

HARRIS, FLOYD O.

50341006 Competition Solos, Book 3 Flute (Grade 3.5)

A practical collection of competition solos for young instrumentalists, many of which are on state festival lists. The piano book includes alternate accompaniments for instruments of different pitch and therefore can be used for any instrument in the book three series. Titles included: Brass Bangles; Caprice; Dancing Silhouettes; Evening in the Country; Ocean Beach (Valse); Polka from Bartered Bride; Viennese Sonata No. 4 (Rondo)

HARRIS, FLOYD/ SIENNICKI, EDMUND

50341005 Competition Solos, Book 2 Flute/Oboe (Grade 2.5)

Book 2 is a practical collection of competition solos, many of which are on state festival lists. Piano book includes alternate accompaniments for instruments of different pitch and therefore can be used for any instrument in the book two series. Titles included: The Young Prince; Viennese Sonatina No. 1 (Allegro); Flower of the Orient; The King's Jester; Two Short Pieces; Spirit of Victory; Barcarolle and Scherzetto; Sparkles; Waltz from Album for the Young.

KERKORIAN, GREGORY M.

50341008 Easy Orginal Flutes Duets and Trios

Beautifully written and arranged with the young player in mind, these duets and trios make wonderful concert and festival repertoire for early performance.

SOLO, UNACCOMPANIED

ADLER, SAMUEL

10410523 Canto XIII for Flute (Grade 4)

Adler, Samuel. Published by Ludwig Music, Cleveland,. Copyright 1994. A rare piece for solo piccolo, this work may be performed straight, or the player may make dramatic entrances and theatrical gestures.

FERROUD, PIERRE OCTAVE

M284891 Three Pieces

SIENNICKI, EDMUND J.

10340101 Recorder Fun (Grade 1)

SOLO WITH PIANO

BACH, J.S.
Marteau, Henri

10410234 Andante Cantabile (Grade 3)

Andante Cantabile [Sinfonia Concertante in E-flat for Two Violins and Orchestra: Andante]

BRICCIALDI, GIULIO
Davis, Albert O.

10410186 Carnival of Venice for Flute and Piano (Grade 4)

This famous melody in theme-and-variations form features a marvelous cadenza. Its technical challenges are dazzlingly impressive!

BUSSER, HENRI

M114291 Petite Suite

M298091 Prelude Et Scherzo

CASELLA, ALFREDO

M266891 Barcarola E Scherzo

M371291 Sicilienne and Burlesque

CHAMINADE, CECILE

M114791 Air De Ballet: Seren

DEBUSSY, CLAUDE

M168591 Clair De Lune

GANNE, LOUIS

M127091 Andante Et Scherzo

GAUBERT, PHILIPPE

M186691 Deux Esquisses

M122791 Nocturne Et Allegro

M196191 Sicilienne: Madrigal

M218391 Sonata In A

M297991 Suite (Grade 4)

This suite, by renowned French flutist Philippe Gaubert, is in four movements, with each movement dedicated to a master flutist of the time. It is a fine contest or recital selection for the advancing musician. Movements: I. Invocation (danse de pretresses), II. Berceuse Orientale, III. Barcarolle, IV. Shzerzo-Valse

GERMAN, EDWARD

M330491 Suite

GLIERE, REINHOLD

M330691 Two Pieces, Op.35

GRIFFES, CHARLES TOMLINSON

M282291 Poeme

HAHN, REYNALDO

M342491 Two Pieces

HARTY, HAMILTON

M292591 In Ireland

HUE, GEORGES

M152191 Fantaisie (Grade 4)

Composed for the Paris Conservatory 1913 and later orchestrated in 1923, Hue's Fantasie is a beautiful work for the advancing flutist. The piece begins with a spacious and atmospheric Assez lent section, which is complimented by intricate melodic lines on the flute. This introduction leads into a beautiful Modere section and concludes with a rousing Tres vif encore.

REINECKE, CARL

W100891 Concerto Op. 283

ROSENHAUS, STEVEN

P001791 Rescuing Psyche

Rescuing Psyche for flute and piano was commissioned by the Music Teachers National Association and the NYSTMA and was premiered by flutist Kelly J. Covert and pianist Nathan Hess. Rescuing Psyche takes its inspiration from Greek mythology. Eros, a god, and Psyche, a mortal, are in love, but Aphrodite is jealous. Aphrodite successfully traps the mortal in a coma, but Eros wakes his love by playing a flute. The flute part has some key clicks and flutters but no other extended techniques or special effects are required.

WIDOR, CHARLES-MARIE

M183591 Suite, Op. 34

TRIO

KOECHLIN, CHARLES

M333291 Three Divertissements

Questions/ comments? info@keiserproductions.com